THE FINE AND DECORATIVE
ART COLLECTIONS OF
BRITAIN AND IRELAND

The National Art-Collections Fund
Book of Art Galleries and Museums

THE FINE AND DECORATIVE ART COLLECTIONS OF BRITAIN AND IRELAND

WRITTEN AND EDITED BY

Jeannie Chapel and Charlotte Gere

WITH AN INTRODUCTION BY SIR JOHN SUMMERSON

PICTURE RESEARCH, SUB-EDITING AND INDEXES BY CAROLINE CUTHBERT,
JANE SHOAF TURNER AND FRANCIS GRAHAM

WEIDENFELD AND NICOLSON

LONDON

A large quarry of heraldic glass with the rebus of
John Islip, d. 1532, Abbot of Westminster, 16thc
(Burrell Collection, Glasgow, Scotland)

Frontispiece: Neptune and Glaucus marble group by
Giovanni Lorenzo Bernini, *c.* 1622
(Victoria and Albert Museum, London)

George Weidenfeld & Nicolson Limited
91 Clapham High Street London sw4

Printed and bound in Italy by L.E.G.O. Vicenza

Contents

Crucifixion attributed to Duccio di Buoninsegna, Sienese, 14thc (Manchester City Art Gallery)

Foreword

THE MARQUIS OF NORMANBY

This book aims to give an idea of the great riches of fine and decorative art in the public museums and galleries of Britain and Ireland. Most people are aware of what they might see in our great national museums, and for many their local museum is known and loved since childhood and has nurtured a life-long love of the arts. However, many of us are unconscious of the wealth of treasures possessed by the smaller museums, or even by the great regional or university museums and galleries. I hope that this book will entice you to investigate these.

For the greater part of this century, since its foundation in 1903, the National Art-Collections Fund has assisted the museums and galleries of the country, and now the houses of the National Trust, to build up their collections, and to retain many of the works of art in danger of being dispersed. Over three hundred museums have benefited from NACF help, and the major part of the illustrations in this book are of works of art acquired with NACF support. Over the years, this has contributed to the transformation of many of our regional museums so that they can now claim to possess collections of international importance.

Our museums and galleries need further resources to provide better displays, conservation and additions to their collections. At a time of rapidly rising prices for increasingly rare works of art of museum quality, the resources required are daunting, as is the task of the NACF in helping to preserve the Nation's treasures.

This book is a first attempt to provide a well illustrated and comprehensive view of the fine and decorative art in our museums and galleries in such a way that the visitor or reader can discover at a glance where, for example, collections of early Italian painting, of sculpture, or 18th-century porcelain or of Art Deco furniture may be found, but its main purpose is to attract you to unknown and unexpected treasures.

This book was made possible by most generous sponsorship from Lex Service plc (and Volvo Concessionaires Ltd), who contributed towards the editorial costs. This sponsorship was supplemented by a grant from the Government. Without these sponsors the book could not have been undertaken and profits will go to the National Art-Collections Fund.

Editorial Note

PHOTOGRAPHIC ACKNOWLEDGEMENTS

The editors wish to thank the following for their permission to reproduce photographs belonging to them: Her Majesty the Queen for gracious permission to use *The Lady with the Virginals and a Gentleman* by Jan Vermeer and *The Vase Bearer* by Andrea Mantegna, all the museums who supplied photographs of their works of art, and the Trustees of the British Museum, the Governors of Dulwich Gallery, the Visitors of the Ashmolean Museum, the Syndics of the Fitzwilliam Museum and Messrs Sothebys.

The painting of the interior of the National Gallery by Giuseppi Gabrielli (see cover) is owned by the Government Art Collection. We would like to thank Dr Wendy Baron, Dr Mary Beal, Mr Jonathan Bourne, Mrs Margaret Clark, Mr Trevor Galloway and Miss Eileen Tweedy for their assistance in obtaining the photograph and for permission to use it.

The Museums which have been included in this necessarily selective book do not include those which are run by the National Trust, the Department of the Environment or other associated bodies. The National Trust already publishes very full information about its properties in which the fine and decorative collections are described. Similarly, most of the others are well served with excellent guidebooks. Largely due to the constrictions of space, regimental museums and collections have been omitted since they are concerned primarily with their own history and therefore the artistic merit of their holdings—often very conspicuous—is incidental. The same is true of the local history collections held by museums throughout the country; where these are mentioned, they are rarely described in any detail. In view of the space limitations which were inevitable in dealing with such a large subject in a single volume, the illustrations and their captions have been used to supplement the text rather than simply to complement it.

The book is divided into three large sections: first London with the museums in alphabetical order by name, e.g. Geffrye Museum comes under 'G'; secondly the provincial museums in alphabetical order by town, and then by alphabetical order of name within each town. Thirdly, Scotland, Wales, Northern Ireland and the Republic of Ireland, starting with Scotland, are arranged in the same way—alphabetically, of towns and names within the towns.

We are grateful to the staff of the museums who have helped us to compile this guide and who have kindly checked our draft entries for errors. While every effort has been made to ensure the greatest possible degree of accuracy, visitors wishing to view a specific work of art are urged to telephone in advance. Opening times in particular are susceptible to seasonal variation and administrative decisions beyond the control of the staff.

Even as we go to press a number of important projects are in the pipeline, and by the time this book appears there may indeed be a firm opening date for the Clore Gallery, which is to house the Turners, bequeathed by the artist to the Nation, but distributed among a number of institutions since his death. No mention has been made of the Tate Gallery in the north, the Sainsbury extension to the National Gallery, or the return of the ethnographical division to the British Museum in Great Russell Street, since plans for these are not yet sufficiently advanced. The status of collections can also change surprisingly rapidly: the acquisition of a gift or bequest can transform a local museum from a primarily archæological and natural history collection into a repository of a significant fine or decorative art collection. Similarly, the very thematic character of, for instance, the Newmarket Collection of Sporting Art or the Pollock's Toy Museum may be transcended by an acquisition of great artistic importance.

Our colleagues at the National Art-Collections Fund office and our museum friends and associates all deserve special thanks for their help and support, as we had constantly to ask for information needing an immediate response. We are particularly grateful for the thoughtful and patient help of Miss Johanna Awdry, our editor at Weidenfeld and Nicolson and to Mr Trevor Vincent, who has realised our vision in his elegant and sympathetic design of the book. Other burdensome demands fell upon the following: Mr Ronald Alley, Mr John Gere, Dr Catherine Gordon, Mr Lionel Lambourne, Mrs Daphne Montgomery, Mr Sean Popplewell, Lady Stevens, Miss Angela Summerfield, Miss Eileen Tweedy, Mr Giles Waterfield, Mrs Frank White and Mr John Woodward. Finally, the credit for inaugurating the whole project must go to Sir Peter Wakefield, Director of the National Art-Collections Fund, whose inspiration it was. His constructive criticism and encouragement—given in approximately equal measure—have been invaluable throughout.

The Architecture of British Museums and Art Galleries

JOHN SUMMERSON

The quest for a 'first' museum or art gallery is likely to be vain, so unstable are the meanings of these expressions. In Britain, there is a good case for calling the old Ashmolean at Oxford 'the first' museum. It was certainly built between 1679 and 1683 for the preservation and public display of the antiquities and curiosities collected by the elder John Tradescant and absorbed into the hoard of Elias Ashmole who presented the whole to the University. It was a purpose-built 'cabinet of curiosities' to which there were earlier parallels on the Continent, but none, it seems, in Britain.

The Ashmolean had no immediate successors. It is not until we come to the 19th century that the word 'museum' comes to be identified with buildings of a peculiar character—buildings with classical Antique references, of a certain solemnity and some pedagogical intention, with almost windowless walls, and mostly lit from the roof. Professor Mordaunt Crook has drawn attention to the original Hunterian Museum at Glasgow, built in 1804 and demolished sixty years later, as an almost forgotten prototype (*The British Museum*, 1972, p. 63). With its Doric portico, its dome, its relief panels in lieu of windows in the upper storey, it was the epitome of much that was to follow.

In England, it might be said that the rear gallery of the Soane Museum, built in 1808, was the first haunt of the enlightened museum spirit. It contained a library, a 'plaister room' and, in the basement, a 'catacomb', and was called a *museum* to distinguish it from the house which Soane, four years later, built in front of it, facing Lincoln's Inn Fields. The gallery is entirely top-lit and the exterior towards Whetstone Park (the narrow back street between Holborn and the north side of Lincoln's Inn Fields) is blind except for attenuated round-headed recesses and a 'primitivist' brick cornice. It is nothing much to look at, but Soane was very self-conscious about it and felt he was creating something.

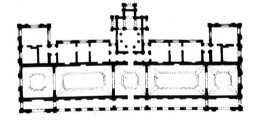

Soane had the real museum mind and it was appropriate that he should have been chosen to design the gallery at Dulwich for which Noel Desenfans left a bequest and which was built in 1811 as an appendage to Dulwich College. It consists of one continuous suite of top-lit galleries, with side rooms which were originally almshouses, and a projecting mausoleum in which the founder's corpse is laid up. The style of architecture is Soane's own. Few liked it at the time and the gallery had no imitators. The next picture gallery to be built in the metropolitan area was the National Gallery in Trafalgar Square.

Dulwich Picture Gallery, with ground plan (Photo: Sir John Soane's Museum)

At this point it is already necessary to take account of the rising tide of middle-class provincial culture—the 'Lit. and Phil.' movement. Many provincial galleries originated as 'Institutions', either 'Literary and Philosophical' or 'Artistic', supported by subscribers. Of these, one of the earliest and architecturally by far the most imposing, was the Royal Institution of Fine Arts at Manchester (now the Manchester City Art Gallery). In 1824 Charles Barry, then aged twenty-nine, won a limited competition for this building, defeating J. B. Papworth, Francis Goodwin, John Foster and Lewis Wyatt. At that point in his career Barry was in the unhappy position of having acquired prime expertise in the Greek and Italian styles but being unprepared for the sudden overwhelming demand for Gothic. He nevertheless won competitions for churches in the Manchester area with rather laboured Gothic designs; these gave him standing in Manchester and admitted him to the Royal Institution competition. For this the appropriate style was the classical, but the interesting thing about Barry's design is that it was not so much English 'Greek Revival' as an essay in 'Modern French', considerably influenced by the published designs of A. L. Dubut. Most of his interiors have been remodelled, but the entrance hall, rising into the externally conspicuous lantern from which it receives its light and surrounded at first floor level by a gallery supported on Doric columns, typifies the spatial sense of the new French school. Its recent redecoration has brought out its delicacy and sense of surface.

In the year before Barry started his Manchester building, the Trustees of the British Museum had approved a design for the total rebuilding of Montagu House in Bloomsbury, where the British Museum had been housed and (nominally at least) accessible to scholars since the Act of 1753. This was a great and innovative national enterprise. The original holdings of the Museum were the Cotton, Harley and Sloane collections, but since 1753 the Trustees had been obliged to accept and store the Towneley collection, the Elgin marbles, George II's library and a great deal else. The building of a structure commensurate with such vast material wealth was inevitable and the Government placed the responsibility in the hands of Robert Smirke. Smirke was one of the Board of Works triumvirate; he and his colleagues Nash and Soane each had his allotted area of responsibility, and Montagu House was in Smirke's. This was fortunate, because Nash was seventy and heading for trouble with Buckingham Palace while the architecture of the sixty-nine-year-old Soane was getting odder and odder. Smirke was only forty-three and at the top of his form; a cool man, well versed in the newly revealed architectural classics of Asia Minor, a great constructor and a faultless administrator.

Smirke has never had quite enough credit for the powerful, lucid, perfectly detailed building which, designed in or before 1823, only reached completion in 1847: the younger generation of the 1840s, watching the laborious erection of the Prienian colonnade when they believed that 'pure Grecian' was over and done with, probably felt a certain understandable nausea. The Museum was 'copyist', 'cold' and 'dead', an indictment that has never been quite extinguished.

The first part of the Museum to be built (1828) was the east wing, containing the King's Library. A Corinthian order rules these great rooms but its columns hide discreetly in recesses, with only the rich entablature running round to support the coffered ceilings and crown the almost continuous revetment of the subtly detailed bookcases. All Smirke's galleries have a strong, thoughtful character. So have the entrance hall and staircase, where a Greek Doric order binds the components into strenuous continuity. Smirke's way of extending the Greek *anta* to the modelling of piers and window-surrounds is much in evidence, and the hall must have been a marvellous spectacle before his polychromatic decoration was obliterated.

Smirke's plan was less successful in the central court which was bleak, almost sunless, and quite useless. Happily, it provided a space for the erection of Panizzi's circular Reading Room whose giant dome of cast iron was designed by Smirke's younger brother Sydney and built in 1854–57.

While the British Museum was slowly rising, nourished by spasmodic Treasury grants, the National Gallery went up fairly quickly between 1834 and 1838 on the north side of what was to become Trafalgar Square. By this time the old Board of Works had been dissolved and the award of the commission to William Wilkins was, it seems, largely the result of the vigorous propaganda he conducted on his own behalf. The building housed in one wing the Angerstein Collection (the nucleus of the National Gallery) and in the other, until its removal to Burlington House in 1866, the Royal Academy of Arts.

The National Gallery's exterior is one of the outstanding non-successes of British architecture. It is a stylistic hybrid and the bits and pieces of which it is made up relate

National Gallery of Scotland, Edinburgh (Photo: Royal Commission on Ancient Monuments, Scotland)

The British Museum, main entrance front (Photo: British Museum)

badly to each other and worse to the whole. The architect who inaugurated the Greek Revival with the perfectionist achievement of Downing College, Cambridge, and who went on to build the museum of the Yorkshire Philosophical Society in the grounds of St Mary's Abbey at York in 1827–30, ought to have done better. The obligatory reuse of the columns from the portico of the demolished Carlton House cannot have made his task easier; and while the steps before the portico are well managed, the dome is a sadly misconceived object which nobody has ever tried to defend.

The failure of the National Gallery marks the collapse of the Greek revival in England. In Scotland it continued to thrive. The Royal Institution on the Mound in Edinburgh, designed by William Playfair in 1822, had more Greek Doric columns than even the Royal High School on Calton Hill and acquired still more when it was lengthened and the portico doubled in 1832. This is the building now occupied by the Royal Scottish Academy. Its companion building on the Mound, the National Gallery of Scotland, was also built by Playfair, but at the end of his life: he just lived to finish it before his death in 1857. The style is Greek Ionic, with two adjacent porticos on the north side, their duality signifying the original joint occupancy of the building. The Royal Scottish Academy had one half and the National Gallery the other. It was not until 1906 that the National Gallery took over the whole building.

1857 is a late date for a 'pure' Greek Revival building, but the Scots were tenacious of neo-classicism and, as we shall see, their tenacity was to have an effect in England. In London, Barry's *cinquecento* had swept the board clear of the Grecian orders, while Pugin's followers were moving in an altogether different direction. The next museums to claim our attention are at the ancient universities—the Fitzwilliam at Cambridge (1836–45) and the new Ashmolean at Oxford (1841–45), and neither can qualify as wholly Greek.

The Fitzwilliam was built from the magnificent bequest of Viscount Fitzwilliam, who not only left the whole of his collection of works of art to the University but in addition more than £100,000 for the erection and maintenance of a museum. With such resources, the British Museum could be outpaced and the National Gallery eclipsed. A competition was held in 1834, for which twenty-seven architects submitted designs. That of George Basevi, then aged forty, was chosen.

Basevi took full advantage of the opportunity for uninhibited exterior display, though it flags a little in the side elevations. He took from Smirke the idea of a continuous colonnade turning abruptly outwards to make an eight-column portico and then going back into line. But Basevi's colonnade is less protracted than Smirke's and has a happier ending: instead of vanishing round the corner, as Smirke's does, it is halted at each end by hollow pavilions whose clustering pilasters give a Baroque sense of depth to the whole frontispiece. The hall and staircase constitute another grandiose set piece; indeed, portico, colonnade and entrance hall between them take up nearly half the total area of the original building. The other half is occupied by the galleries, those on the main floor being top-lit. Basevi was a pupil of Soane and if one looks for the old man's influence it is found in the lantern-light of Gallery III, where a second lantern rides on top of the first as do Soane's lights in the Westminster Law Courts.

After Basevi's fatal fall from a scaffold at Ely Cathedral in 1845, C. R. Cockerell took over and altered the staircase design, introducing the barrel-vaulted bays over the side galleries—an imaginative borrowing from Wren's church in Piccadilly.

At Oxford we meet Cockerell again, in the building commonly known as the Ashmolean which is entirely of his design. It consists, in fact, of two buildings. The block towards St Giles contains the Taylorian Institute for foreign languages provided for in the bequest of the well-known architect and Sheriff of the City of London, Sir Robert Taylor, who died in 1788. The corresponding block on the south is part of the Museum and the two are linked by a lower block, forming a gallery of antiquities, with a central four-column portico. This was felt to be an unusual and controversial disposition, and critical opinion is divided on the merits of this curious building. Russell Hitchcock, who calls the plan incoherent, is shocked by the competing Greek and Italian cornices and the 'unbelievably awkward' junction of the low centre and high end blocks. David Watkin defends this last feature as a deliberate gesture of 'dislocation' and quotes with approval Fergusson's verdict on the whole building: 'There is perhaps no building in England on which the refined student of architecture can dwell with so much pleasure, there is not a moulding or chisel mark anywhere which is not the result of deep study, guided by refined feeling' (*The Life and Work of C. R. Cockerell, RA*, 1974, p. xix). Cockerell perceived a subtle affinity between the Grecian profiles he had

Montrose Museum, Scotland (Photo: Royal Commission on Ancient Monuments, Scotland)

been discovering and those characteristic of certain kinds of Italian Mannerism; the brilliant play of these two apparently opposed modes amply justifies Fergusson's enthusiasm.

Both the Fitzwilliam and the Ashmolean were substantially completed in 1845. There followed a period when few museums were built, and when their social function was being critically examined. In 1845 Parliament passed an 'Act for enabling Town Councils to establish Public Museums of Art and Science'. The purpose of such museums was not academic but 'for the instruction and entertainment of the inhabitants'. The bill had been introduced by William Ewart, an advanced Liberal who had been associated with the Report of 1836 which led to the creation of the Government Schools of Design. It was strongly supported by Joseph Hume, the radical Member of Parliament for Montrose where, as it happened, a most elegant little museum had been built in 1836.

This Act, which enabled local authorities to purchase land, erect buildings and accept gifts for museum purposes, imposed a condition that entry to public museums should not exceed one penny. It was superseded by the Act of 1850 which insisted that entry should be free; and it was the adoption of this latter Act which enabled so many towns and cities to receive benefactions in the shape of museums and galleries and maintain them out of the rates. One of the first rate-maintained museums was at Warrington in Lancashire. Created by Warrington's first mayor on the premises of the Warrington Natural History Society, it was given a site by a wealthy citizen. The still standing, neat, classical building is after a design by the famous John Dobson of Newcastle, executed in a simplified form in 1855. In the following year Liverpool moved in the same direction, accepting the gift of a library and museum at the hands of Alderman William Brown. A competition was held, the winner being Thomas Allom, better known as a draughtsman than an architect. His building (now the Merseyside County Museum) has a six-column Corinthian portico echoing, rather shyly, the majesty of St George's Hall across the road.

Most museums up to 1860 were in some version of the classical (the Tudor Gothic museum at Saffron Walden, 1834, is a curious exception). The first serious departure was caused by a competition held by the University of Oxford in 1854 for a Museum of Physical Sciences. Although this was not a museum of art, no museum ever made a greater stir in the art world of its time than the building which emerged as the winner, the work of the Dublin partnership, Deane and Woodward. There was nothing romantic or spectacular about this quiet, symmetrical building with its low central tower and its flavour of Ruskin's *The Stones of Venice*. What was controversial was the courtyard behind the main block which was covered in iron and glass—an equivalent of Gothic in 19th-century technology. The Oxford Museum was what the Ruskinians and the Pre-Raphaelites were looking for and *Building News* did not hesitate to name it 'the greatest civil building of our day'. It was completed in 1858.

The Oxford Museum's influence on museum design was not very extensive. It can be traced perhaps in the Royal Albert Memorial Museum at Exeter, for which a competition was held in 1869, and which is the best example of a Gothic museum of the 'high' revival period. Planned to contain a school of art and a free library as well as a museum, it is a polychrome affair in brick and stone and has a grand staircase with a statue of Prince Albert in a niche on the first landing. The designer was a local man, John Hayward. A better piece of Gothic is (Sir) Gilbert Scott's Albert Institute at Dundee, built as a 'Lit. and Phil.' in 1865–69. This has a distinct likeness to the Oxford Museum but is more elaborate and vigorous in its detail and is remarkable for the Gothic reinterpretation of the Renaissance perron leading to the first floor.

Few museums and galleries of later years attempted the Gothic, but G. R. Crickmay's modest County Museum building at Dorchester, 1881–83, with gables, battlements and a brave assortment of windows, deserves a mention. On a different level altogether is the John Rylands Library at Manchester, 1890–1910, the queen of all secular Gothic buildings in Britain of the 1890s. It is more of a library than a museum or gallery and, with its vaulted nave, aisle passages and clerestory, is more of a church than either; which, after all, is appropriate to John Rylands's main interests which were theology and early printed bibles. The architect was Basil Champneys.

From about 1860 the lead in museum design and construction was taken by South Kensington. The South Kensington story is long and complicated and is recorded with admirable lucidity in Vol. 38 of the *Survey of London*. We shall not attempt even to summarise it here, merely offering some observations on the kind of architecture it produced. The earliest architectural creations on the Government's South Kensington property were sponsored by the Department of Science and Art, set up in 1852 and directed by (Sir) Henry Cole. Until

Natural History Museum, main entrance
(Photo: RIBA Drawings Collection, B.A.L.)

1884 this department was responsible for all designing at South Kensington and it developed a style which, whenever it is found, is clearly recognizable as the 'South Kensington' style. It is basically engineering (mostly in iron) with an *appliqué* of sculptural ornament, sometimes of high quality, and a tendency to adopt architectural forms deriving from North Italian Renaissance models. Terracotta and ceramics were favoured materials. The Gothic/classic dilemma is evaded by placing both styles under tribute. The style may be seen today in the South Court (1862) of the Victoria and Albert and in the buildings surrounding the Quadrangle. Outside London it may be seen in two buildings erected by the Department: the Royal Scottish Museum in Chambers Street, Edinburgh and, in exceptionally palatial form, at the National Gallery, Dublin.

The originator of the 'South Kensington' style cannot be very precisely named but the leader of the group of artists who produced it was certainly Captain Francis Fowke. He was an officer in the Royal Engineers and in so far as he was an architect was self-taught. Cole's strong prejudice against professional architects rendered the collaboration successful, especially since Fowke seems to have been a sympathetic and intelligent collaborator with artists and craftsmen.

The Museum of Art was not the only cultural institution claiming accommodation in the South Kensington precinct. The British Museum's vast accumulation of Natural History specimens required a home where it could expand and where the didactic ideas of (Sir) Richard Owen could be promoted. The buildings housing the Exhibition of 1862 were considered but dismissed as unworthy, and the site was given over to two joint projects—a Natural History Museum and a Museum of Patents. For these two purposes a vast palace was envisaged and a competition organised. Fowke, who had designed the original Exhibition buildings, entered for the competition and, to nobody's surprise—except allegedly the assessors'—won it with a design in the North Italian Renaissance style, with French-type pavilions and a good many domes.

But in the following year Fowke died, at the early age of forty-two. The question at once arose whether his design should be executed and if so by whom. Doubts were resolved when Alfred Waterhouse accepted the invitation to erect Fowke's building but with ample latitude to revise not only the plans but also the elevations. The proposal for a Museum of Patents was dropped and the project became more manageable. Waterhouse decided to alter the style

Victoria and Albert Museum, the quadrangle in 1878
(Photo: Victoria and Albert Museum)

from 15th-century North Italian Renaissance to 12th-century German Romanesque. He removed the central element with its clustered domes and replaced it with a Romanesque Cathedral 'west front' with twin towers and a great portal. In spite of these ruthlessly radical 'revisions', a good deal of Fowke's work still remains in the design and disposition of the pavilions, in the general pattern of the fenestration, and even in some decorative details. It could be said that much that seems, and indeed is, original in the present building is the result of the re-thinking of Fowke's Renaissance in terms of Waterhouse's Romanesque.

The Natural History Museum was by far the largest and most impressive building, apart from the British Museum, to be built for museum purposes in Britain. It was well received and its architect became the most respected as well as the most affluent of British practitioners, constantly in request not only as executant but also as assessor in architectural competitions— a capacity in which he was exceedingly influential.

Outside London the pace of museum-building increased from the 1860s onwards. At least seven went up in the 1870s, twice that number in the 1880s, and twenty at least in the 1890s. Thereafter numbers declined. In the ascendant years no very distinct types emerged either in style or arrangement. To local councillors art was always in itself slightly suspect and was felt to be best dealt with in combination with some practical purpose like a library or a school of art or science, or some other municipal enterprise. Moreover, the fact that neither a picture gallery nor a museum could be justified unless there was something to put inside it required a benefactor who had something ready to hand. The architecturally significant museums and galleries are those that were dependent on the gift of a substantial and worthwhile collection.

The 1870s saw the erection of museums at Blackburn, Liverpool (the Walker Art Gallery), Derby, Southport, York and Sunderland, all except York finding their architects through competition. The York Gallery, designed by Edward Taylor in 1879, is memorable for its quaintly detailed Florentine loggia, but the most gloriously independent freak of the 1870s is the Bowes Museum at Barnard Castle. This is a colossal French château designed in the late 1860s by a French architect, originally for a site near Calais but hastily re-sited in Co. Durham when war threatened on the Continent. The founders were John Bowes of Streatlam and his French wife, Joséphine. The architect was Pellechet. A latter-day Château-de-Maisons in the Tees valley is a wonderfully improbable event but most assuredly welcome. How one wishes that more English architects of the 1870s had had the technical competence of Pellechet.

The last two decades of Queen Victoria's reign saw the foundation of many of the principal museum and gallery buildings in London and the provinces. Thus, in chronological order, we have Ipswich, 1875–81; Birmingham, 1881–85; Preston (Harris), 1882; Wolverhampton, 1884; Sheffield (Mappin), 1887; Leeds, 1886–88; London (Tate), 1892; Manchester (Whitworth), 1894–1900; London (National Portrait Gallery), 1896. Nearly all these buildings are classical, in the broad sense of the word. None are defiantly non-classical but a few escape in a non-committal 'Renaissance'. Wolverhampton is still in the Barry tradition, while Ipswich pins its faith to Norman Shaw. In quality of design there are wide variations and architectural competence does not always correspond with worthy social intentions.

The Birmingham story is a case in point. The century's best governed and most progressive city had not, up to 1880, done much about art. But in that year came a challenge. George and Richard Tangye, the industrial engineers, offered £5,000 for the purchase of works of art if the Corporation would at once take measures to build an art gallery and a further £5,000 if a similar sum were publicly subscribed. The challenge was accepted. The Corporation, under its ambitious mayor, Joseph Chamberlain, had lately acquired the local gas company and the gas offices required accommodation. A site adjoining the recently built Council House was therefore acquired in the joint interests of gas and art. Gas below, art above: a nice model of the fruits of industry supporting the achievements of the imagination.

The architecture in Colmore Row and Chamberlain Square reflects the story. We have the energetic, ebullient, slightly amateurish façade of the Council House with its pompous centrepiece dome and sculptured pediments, the work of the Birmingham architect Yeoville Thomason. Turning the corner we find the Art Gallery continuing the design but dignified by a double portico. Perched on the Edmund Street corner is a rather absurd clock-tower with a red tile roof. The architecture is not of the quality of Barry at Manchester or Elmes at Liverpool but it has an unembarrassed jollity which exactly matches the mood of Birmingham in the 1880s.

Preston presents an altogether different picture. The Harris Museum and Art Gallery is

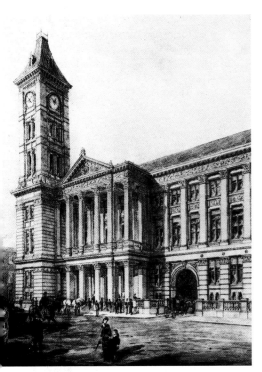

Birmingham, City Art Gallery & Museum
(Photo: Birmingham, City Art Gallery & Museum)

The Tate Gallery (Photo: The Tate Gallery)

one of the most striking monuments of the Greek Revival, but it happens to have been built forty years after the Revival was over. It is an almost incredible anachronism. Little is known of its architect James Hibbert, except that he was a Preston alderman who eventually filled the office of mayor. He seems to have taken the view in 1882 that nothing serious had happened in architecture for forty years. Nor did he feel it necessary to adopt ideas outside his own county: his exterior elevations, at least, can be accounted for in terms of Manchester and Liverpool monuments. Nevertheless, this building has an irresistible vitality of its own.

The Mappin Art Gallery at Sheffield looks like another belated survival. Designed in 1886 by the very able Sheffield architects, Flockton and Gibbs, it is as Greek as it can be but somehow not strictly in the 'Greek Revival' taste. It has more the air of a genteel imitation of von Klenze's work in Munich.

Then there is the Tate Gallery. It is difficult to fit this building into the British classical tradition. It seems to have come about in a curiously muddle-headed way, but the fact is that it is one of the first specimens of the new kind of classicism that was making itself felt in competition-entries from about 1890 that was in full flood by the turn of the century, and which is usually miscalled 'Edwardian Baroque'. In 1890 Henry Tate, the sugar magnate, offered his collection of modern British art to the Nation with a gallery to contain it provided that the Government would give the site. Eventually the site of the Millbank Penitentiary was made available and the offer accepted. No competition was held and the commission was put in the hands of thirty-three-year-old Sydney R. J. Smith, of whom nobody had ever heard but who had for some years been associated with Henry Tate. Tate had come to live at Streatham and had found an outlet for his philanthropic instincts in the free library movement which the Lambeth vestry was trying to promote. By 1888 one library had been built by the Vestry, at Knights Hill, of which Smith was the architect. It is still there: a tiny building, plain inside but equipped externally with a two-storey loggia, ornaments in a rich variety of styles and materials, carved heads of great writers and a heavy French roof. That library was paid for out of the rates, but the next, in South Lambeth Road, was the gift of Henry Tate who went on to present three more, all with Smith as architect. It was natural, therefore, that Tate should invite Smith to make sketches for the Gallery of British Art.

The first published design for the British Gallery is the sad little elevation reproduced in the *Building News* for 1892: an unpromising five-part classical building with a glass dome over the centre block and loggias extended along the wings. Then, in 1893, comes a well-drawn perspective by C. W. English of something altogether different. There are now seven domes: five grouped together in the centre (rather like a Russian church) and one on each of the end pavilions. A section shows the beginnings of something like the executed design. After this, Smith was put to a great deal of trouble and suffered much disappointment. The executed design, we are told, 'was the fifth made by the architect, each successive design revealing a shearing-off of projecting members and of purely ornamental features, owing to the paramount necessity felt by many for an even distribution of the masses of building so as to ensure the maximum of light'. The cruellest sacrifice was the lopping off of the high central dome.

After all the shearings and loppings we are left with a plausible if not very refined classical building which has a faintly Beaux-Arts flavour. Sydney Smith's architectural pilgrimage from Knights Hill to Millbank was hard going and earned him little credit; and when Duveen's offer of a new Turner Gallery was accepted in 1908 the Office of Works took the project over without even bothering to consult him.

The other major gallery to be built in London before 1900 was the National Portrait Gallery. The finance was provided by a benefactor, W. H. Alexander, who was presumably responsible for choosing the architect, Ewan Christian: a curious choice in view of the fact that Christian had spent his long life building almost nothing but Gothic churches. Part of the Gallery was necessarily a continuation of Wilkins's National Gallery, and this Christian handled with discretion. For the north block, however, facing up Charing Cross Road, he reverted to 15th-century Florence. The very queer spacing of the upper windows detracts from what would have been a noble mass, in the Medici spirit but with a leaning to the Romanesque.

We must now turn again to the great South Kensington enterprises. The Natural History Museum was opened in 1881, but the Art Museum was at a standstill. It was not until 1890 that the Government decided to complete it and to select the architect by limited competition. Once again the problem of style arose. There was a growing desire to return to academic classicism and John Belcher's spectacular Baroque design was much applauded. Other

The Horniman Museum
(Photo: The Horniman Museum)

competitors felt their way gingerly to something still safely 'Renaissance' but moving in a classical direction. A factor which had some bearing on the choice of style was that the assessor was Alfred Waterhouse whose own Natural History Museum would form a group with the new museum. The only entrant who took this requirement seriously was the young Aston Webb, and it was he who won the competition. His design was diabolically clever, for it succeeded in capturing the feel of Waterhouse's building without overtly imitating it: Renaissance but without columns or pilasters, woven into it were various Waterhousean elements, including a type of traceried window which Waterhouse had taken from Fowke.

Between the winning of the competition and the start of the building eight years elapsed. Changes of various kinds were imposed and Webb himself had many second thoughts, especially about the Cromwell Road façade. In the competition design the entrance was in the base of a modest central tower. By 1899 the tower had vanished and a hugely elaborate portal—a Renaissance equivalent of what Waterhouse had done at the Natural History Museum—had taken its place. Above this rose an attic storey which somehow resolved itself into a podium supporting an enormous quasi-lantern tower of two storeys. This seems to have been inspired by the Certosa at Pavia; at the very top, however, comes a 'crown spire' paraphrasing the uniquely British examples at Newcastle-upon-Tyne, Edinburgh and Aberdeen.

Aston Webb's reputation has not been enhanced in recent reappraisals of the architecture of the early 1900s. He was enormously clever, a marvellous blender of styles, and he executed a vast number of national buildings; but he rarely succeeds in touching the imagination. At the Victoria and Albert by far the most appealing feature is the handling of the two staircases, each contained within an open-arched 'cage' of masonry, brilliantly modelled and providing a series of perspectives of considerable charm. Of the other galleries it is difficult to find much to say that is kind.

The opening of the Victoria and Albert by Edward VII in 1909 rounded off a decade of more architectural excitement in museum and gallery building. It was the decade of the Free Style flutter as well as of Neo-Georgian consolidation and Baroque adventure. 'Free Style' is the term by which we must describe the two galleries designed by C. Harrison Townsend at the turn of the century—the Whitechapel Art Gallery and the Horniman Museum at Forest Hill (both finished in 1901). Internally, both buildings provide simple, practical answers to problems of display. Outside, they are straining to tell us something new, which is (or was) that architecture can have a life of its own, independent of 'the styles'. The idea did not really catch on in 1901 and Harrison's buildings immediately became museum pieces, which they still are, their value enhanced by time and a better appreciation of what was really what at the turn of the century.

The new classicism had got its foot in the door by 1900, so that a building like Glasgow's Kelvingrove Gallery, a dazzling mix of French and Spanish Renaissance which won the competition of 1891, found itself out of date even before it was built. The architects, John W. Simpson and E. J. Milner Allen, promptly changed their style and won the Cartwright Hall, Bradford, competition of 1903 with a design characterised by a Baroque silhouette and much solemn fun with rustication. The assessor in both events was Alfred Waterhouse, as capable as anybody else of moving with the times. In 1905 came the Bristol Art Gallery, presented to the City by the tobacco millionaire, Sir W. H. Wills, with his relative, Frank Wills (later Sir Frank, Lord Mayor of Bristol) as the architect. This was another Baroque explosion, technically weak but making an effective exclamation at the top of Park Street.

The one incontestible masterpiece of the decade is the Edward VII gallery on the north side of the British Museum, begun in 1905 and completed in 1914. It is the work of John James Burnet, a Glaswegian whose native genius was disciplined by a Paris training. It was inevitable that the new rear elevation of the Museum should answer Smirke's colonnaded front with something of comparable scale and splendour. Burnet's order is Ionic, but of a slightly more plastic kind than Smirke's. And it is not free but attached at either end to a 'battered' pylon which it just overlaps, while an attic storey connects the two pylons, above and behind the order. There is more here of Schinkel than of Smirke, and also something of Paris and something of 'Greek' Thomson, all fitted together with the greatest care and subtlety (e.g. the axes of the tapering columns are slightly tilted inwards so that the flutes are vertical where they die into the wall). A strong dramatic touch is the entrance feature which, instead of being emphasised to make an impression, is deliberately understated to remind the visitor of his own insignificance in the presence of the achievements of the past.

In 1910 came the competition for the National Museum of Wales, with Aston Webb, Burnet and Edwin T. Hall as assessors. This was not only an important building in itself but was to be sited in Cardiff's Cathays Park, next to E. A. Rickards's sensationally successful City Hall completed in 1904. In contrast to Rickards's Baroque virtuosity, the winners of the Museum competition, Dunbar Smith and Cecil Brewer, took a sober neo-classical line, with a shapely plan and simple detailing. The transatlantic influence of McKim, Mead and White probably accounts for this as it does also for the classicism of the Lady Lever Art Gallery at Port Sunlight which William and Segar Owen designed for Viscount Leverhulme a few years later. Both the Welsh Museum and the Port Sunlight Gallery were interrupted by the War, the latter being opened in 1922 and the former not until 1927.

American influence pervaded the inter-war years and is found in the Ferens Gallery at Hull (S. N. Cooke, 1927) and in a Georgianised form in the Williamson Gallery at Birkenhead (Hannaford and Thearle, 1938) and also in the new additions to the British Museum and the Tate Gallery, both presented by Lord Duveen and designed by the American Russell Pope.

The Science Museum and the Geological Museum at South Kensington belong to this period. Essentially they are plain concrete carcases, screened from the street by Portland stone façades in a style of architecture which a President of the R.I.B.A. once appropriately described as 'stale chocolate'.

Two spirited inter-war buildings are worth a mention. One is Sir Reginald Blomfield's Usher Gallery at Lincoln, designed to house a small private collection made over to the City by James Ward Usher. Built in 1927, it is one of Blomfield's most personal works, a piece of Francophil design with, as always, a very strong English accent.

The second building, the Barber Institute at Birmingham University, is something altogether different, combining the functions of an art gallery and a postgraduate school of art history. This was a new type of institution, inviting fresh architectural ideas. In the 1930s, when the Barber Trust appointed Thomas Bodkin as director and Robert Atkinson as architect they looked for original thought from both these professionals and it was forthcoming. Atkinson's unusual plan, with the auditorium locked into a square of galleries, the projecting lecture theatre and off-centre entrance, put conventional classicism out of the question. Atkinson adopted a kind of Anglo-Swedish classic, allowing complete freedom of movement while retaining traditional elements and the use of traditional building materials. The Barber Institute represents better than almost any other building (except, perhaps, the R.I.B.A. in Portland Place) the spirit of English architecture in the 1930s.

Since the Second World War between twenty and thirty new museums have been built in Britain. Some have been so discreetly merged with existing buildings as hardly to deserve the epithet 'new' and very few indeed stand out as memorable pieces of architecture in their

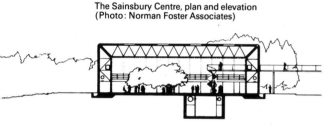

The Sainsbury Centre, plan and elevation
(Photo: Norman Foster Associates)

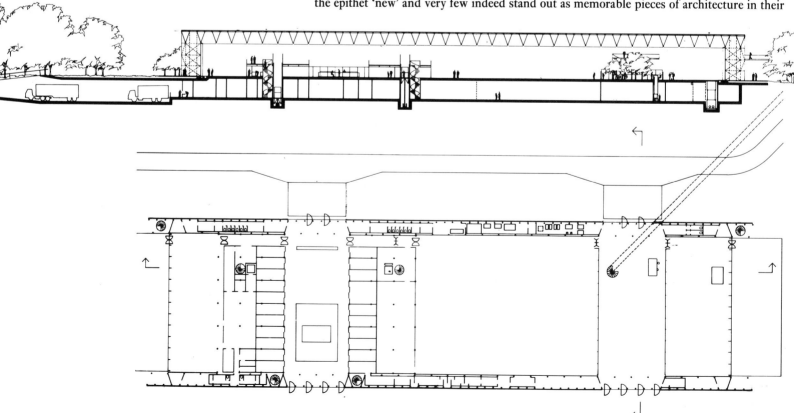

The Burrell Collection (Photo: Barry Gasson Architects)

own right. There is no modern equivalent of the Fitzwilliam at Cambridge or of Glasgow's Kelvingrove Gallery. This is, no doubt, as it should be. We have not lost the feeling generated by the Modern Movement, the sense of withdrawal from architectural exhibitionism and of limiting the architect's function to the protection and display of the exhibits. In practice it can, of course, never be simply left at that; however much the architect may pursue the anonymous and the negative, he is placing on the ground a positive statement which will be judged as architecture.

In the past ten years two remarkable buildings have been built illustrating the museum and gallery problem as it is seen by two different kinds of modern architect. One is the Sainsbury Centre at the University of East Anglia by Norman Foster and the other the Burrell Museum at Glasgow by Barry Gasson. Both are intended to house gifts by wealthy collectors, one to a university, the other to a city, and in both cases the buildings were part of the gift and intended to enclose and service the donors' collections rather than to attract additional works of art. Their functions are not exactly similar: the Sainsbury includes a pedagogical element associated with a Department of Art History (as in the Barber Institute), while the aim of the Burrell is more in line with the purpose broadly defined in the 1845 Act, 'the instruction and entertainment of the inhabitants'. The Sainsbury has an exhibition area with a flexible arrangement of screens; the Burrell is designed more as a close-fitting shell into which some of the exhibits are incorporated. Nevertheless, they are near enough in general purpose to admit legitimate comparison of their respective approaches to design. The Sainsbury has become the most celebrated British example of 'High Tech.', which is to say that the architect's approach has been through engineering and industrial techniques rather than the traditional repertory of the building trades. The Burrell, on the other hand, tends to exploit the values inherent in natural materials and traditional methods of construction.

The Sainsbury Centre looks at first sight like an aircraft hangar, being in effect a long rectangular shed of steel construction with external and internal cladding, arbitrarily sited on the perimeter of the university buildings. It does not immediately declare its purpose nor seduce the eye, and it is only when the interior has been explored that its spatial relationships and sensitive precision of detail begin to be appreciated. The Burrell is more relaxed; its plan derives from a comfortable relationship with the site and it invites leisured movement through its various elements. A feature of both is a consciousness of their natural environment. At the Sainsbury, both ends of the 'hangar' are glazed and the landscape is a living picture filling the whole structural frame. At the Burrell nature draws alongside—a forest scene on the north and a meadow on the south are glimpsed at intervals. The buildings represent two different approaches to the enjoyment of art and nature and neither approach is wrong.

To these two approaches we may add a third which will be illustrated by the Clore Gallery at the Tate, now under construction. This seems likely to challenge the policy of self-effacement and withdrawal seen in so many modern galleries. James Stirling's design is nothing if not positive: a witty, paradoxical, irresponsibly good-humoured creation—a museum piece in its own right. The Turner paintings will be perfectly at liberty to speak for themselves, but the building itself is not going to be excluded from the dialogue with which the visitor will be entertained. It is an imaginative endeavour to make architecture, once again, something more than an envelope of space, to make the solid eloquent: in short, to render the Gallery as critically challenging as the material it contains. There does not seem much wrong with that.

Museum Location Maps

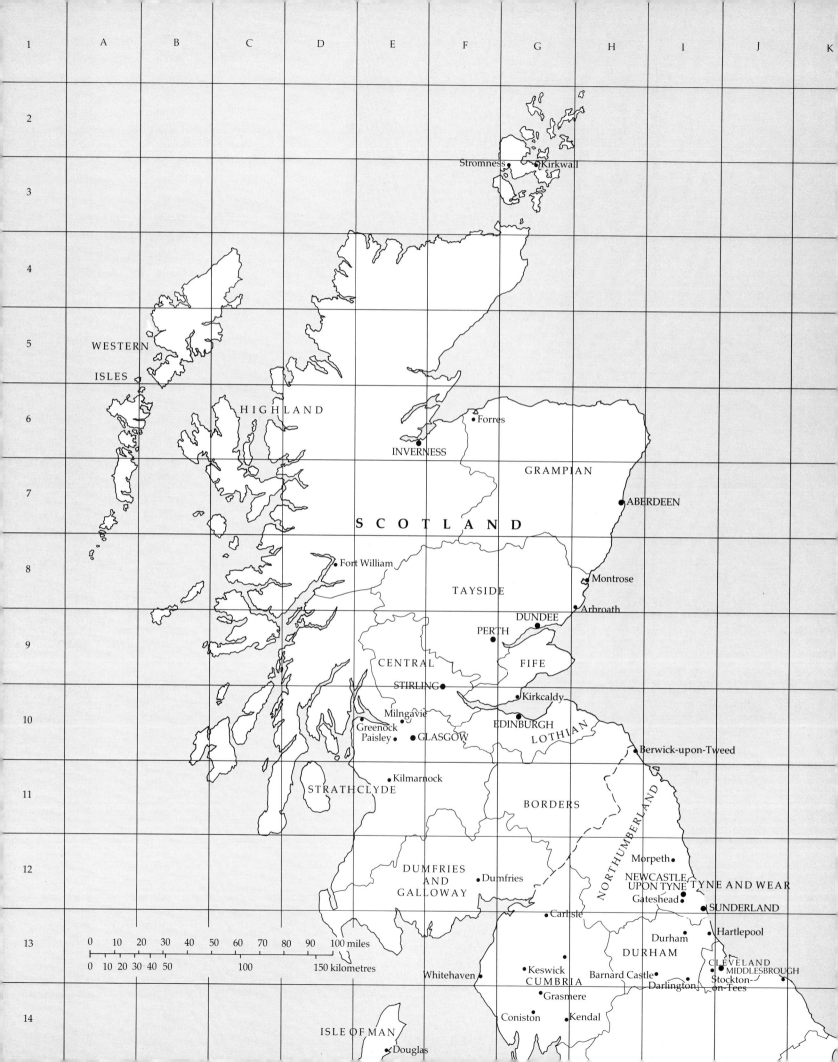

B C D E F G H I J K

1
2
3
4

Letterkenny ●

DONEGAL   LONDONDERRY   ANTRIM   5

Donegal ●   TYRONE

                                    BELFAST ●

N O R T H E R N   6
        I R E L A N D

        FERMANAGH (MONAGHAN

Sligo ●   DOWN
                Enniskillen ●
SLIGO   LEITRIM   ARMAGH

                                        7
MAYO   CAVAN   LOUTH

        ROSCOMMON   LONGFORD

                        WESTMEATH   MEATH   8

GALWAY

                OFFALY   DUBLIN

R E P U B L I C   ● DUBLIN   9

        O F   LEIX   KILDARE   WICKLOW

CLARE   I R E L A N D

                                        10
        ● LIMERICK

LIMERICK   TIPPERARY   KILKENNY   CARLOW

                                WEXFORD   11

                WATERFORD

KERRY   C O R K   12

        CORK ●

0 10 20 30 40 50 60 70 80 90 100 miles   13

0 10 20 30 40 50   100   150 kilometres

                                        14

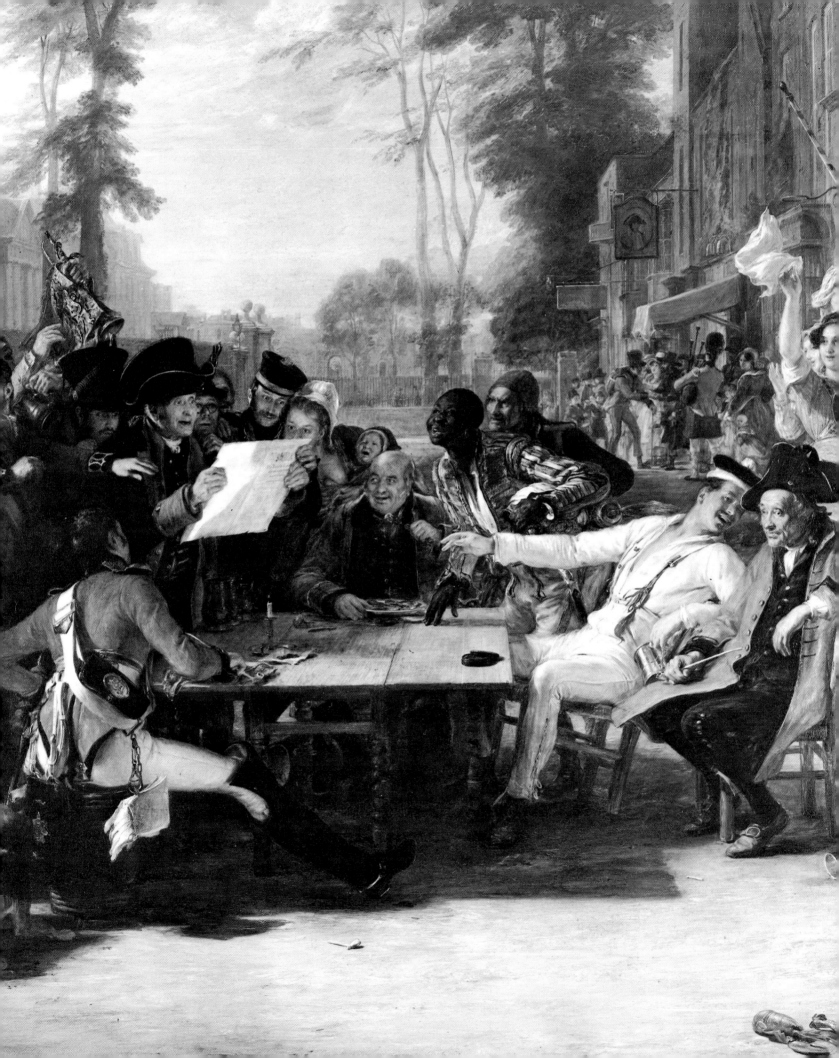

Greater London

Apsley House, The Wellington Museum

London residence of the 1st Duke of Wellington (1769–1852) with contents and other associated items.

European Paintings (17thC–19thC), porcelain and silver (19thC)

Apsley House, 149 Piccadilly, London W1 tel. 01-499 5676

Tues–Thurs, Sat 10–6 pm; Sun 2–6 pm

Admission charge

Apsley House was opened as a museum to the public in 1952. Originally known as 'No. 1 London', being the first house after passing through the Knightsbridge toll gate, it was built by Robert Adam (1728–92) for Henry Bathurst, Baron Apsley, in 1771–78. It was purchased in 1807 by the Marquess Wellesley, who employed the architects James Wyatt (1746–1813) and Thomas Cundy (1765–1825) to make improvements. In 1817 he in turn sold Apsley House to his brother, the Duke of Wellington, who in 1828–29 employed Benjamin Dean Wyatt (1775–1850) and Philip Wyatt (d. 1836) to face the house with Bath stone and add the portico, pediment and extension on the west side.

The 2nd Duke of Wellington first opened the house to the public, three days a week after written application, from 1853. The house and its contents were presented to the Nation by the 7th Duke in 1947. Since 1976, when the Department of Furniture and Woodwork at the Victoria and Albert Museum took over responsibility, it has been restored as near as possible to its appearance during the 1st Duke's time. Detailed watercolours of the interiors executed by Thomas Shotter Boys in the 1850s greatly helped in returning the house to its former glory.

The interiors are particularly fine: remaining from the Adam period are the marvellous decorated staircase, the Piccadilly Drawing Room and the Portico Room. The original plasterwork by Bernasconi and George Jackson & Sons, the metalwork supplied by J. Bramah & Sons and the furniture by Thomas Dowbiggin & Co. also survive.

The plate and china have now been rearranged in a room in the south-west corner of the house in new showcases, which contain, for example, the huge Wellington Shield designed by Thomas Stothard c. 1822 and two magnificent candelabra by Benjamin Smith of 1816–17, all of which were presented to the Duke by the Merchants and Bankers of the City of London. Of special note from the outstanding collection of Sèvres is the famous and recently acquired Egyptian dessert service of 1809–12, consisting of an impressive centrepiece in hard-paste porcelain mounted on *tôle peinte*, based on the Temples of Karnak, Dendera and Philae, and thirty other pieces. Made for the Empress Josephine's divorce present, it was refused by her and given by Louis XVIII to the Duke of Wellington in 1818. Also to be seen is the extensive Prussian service made at the Berlin factory in 1816–19 with sixty-four plates illustrating the Duke's achievements, as well as pieces from the Saxon service of Meissen porcelain and the Austrian service of Vienna porcelain. A large number of silver parcel gilt items from the Deccan service and two silver centrepieces by Paul Storr of 1810–11 and 1811–12 are on display, as are the Duke's many Orders, including the famous diamond-set George from the Order of the Garter, and a number of gold and silver snuff boxes, swords and daggers and other mementoes.

In the staircase hall is one of the house's most memorable works, the over-life-size—more than eleven feet high—nude statue by Canova, of Napoleon holding in his hand a gilt statuette of Victory, made in 1802–10 and installed in 1817, having been rejected by Napoleon. It was purchased by the British Government and given to the Duke by the Prince Regent.

The collection of paintings is essentially a magnificent private one, with very good Dutch and Flemish pictures, including works by Paul Bril, Teniers the Younger, Elsheimer, Nicolaes Maes, Jan Steen, Pieter de Hooch, Wouvermans, etc., many of which are hung in the Piccadilly Drawing Room.

Among the portraits by French artists on view in the Portico Drawing Room are those by Robert Lefèvre of *Pope Pius VII*, 1805, and *Pauline Bonaparte* and *Empress Josephine*, both of 1806; *Joseph Bonaparte* by Gérard and additional portraits by Lefèvre are among the paintings hung in the Yellow Drawing Room.

By far the most impressive group of paintings is in the Waterloo Gallery, which has been rehung to reflect the original arrangement of the paintings as recorded in an 1852 watercolour by John Nash. The Gallery was designed in 1828 by Benjamin Dean Wyatt for the Duke's collection of paintings, many of which, including works by Rubens and Mengs, came into his possession after the Battle of Vitoria, 1813. Some 200 canvases (removed from their stretchers and rolled up) had been taken from the Spanish Royal Collections by Joseph Bonaparte, then King of Spain, and were discovered by the Duke when the King's coach was stopped on fleeing the country. Learning of their royal provenance in 1814, the Duke

Sèvres porcelain *Sucrier* from the 'Egyptian' service designed by Jean-Charles-Nicholas Brachard, 1810–12 (Apsley House)

Opposite] David Wilkie, detail from *Chelsea Pensioners reading the Waterloo Despatch*, 1822 (Apsley House)

Joseph Nash, watercolour of *The Waterloo Gallery*, 1852

Marble statue of Napoleon I holding a figure of Victory by Antonio Canova, 1802 (Apsley House)

not only had the pictures restored but also offered to return them to the new King of Spain, who, though grateful for the gesture, refused to deprive the Duke of what he had acquired by honourable means. Of particular importance are the Velasquez *The Waterseller of Seville*, *c*. 1620, and the wonderful small Correggio *Agony in the Garden*, *c*. 1525, which is said to have been the Duke's favourite painting. By contrast, the Duke disliked Goya's *Equestrian Portrait* of him and thus kept it stored during his lifetime. The three large portraits above the chimneypieces, *Charles I* by Van Dyck, *The Emperor Rudolf II* by Hans von Aachen and *Queen Mary Tudor* after Antonio Mor, have elaborate frames designed by Wyatt. Other fine portraits in the house include the *1st Marquess of Anglesey* by Lawrence of 1818 and Wilkie's *George IV* of 1830 and *William IV* of 1833. Also of interest are *Chelsea Pensioners Reading the Waterloo Despatch*, 1822, by Wilkie, and *The Battle of Waterloo, 1815* by Sir William Allan of 1843.

Displayed in the Dining Room on the mahogany table is a massive centrepiece in silver and silver-gilt from the Portuguese service designed by D. A. de Sequeira for the Duke of Portugal and made in Lisbon in 1812–16. It stretches the full length of the twenty-six-foot table, and originally the dancing figures lining the edge were joined by swags of silk flowers.

Apsley House has an Association of Friends. There is a shop in the hall, which sells an excellent guidebook by Simon Jervis and Maurice Tomlin, published in 1984.

Bethnal Green Museum of Childhood

Toys, games, dolls, dolls' houses, puppets and children's costume

Cambridge Heath Road, London E2
tel. 01-980 2415/3204/4315

Mon–Thurs, Sat 10–5.50 pm; Sun 2.30–5.50 pm. Closed Fri

Admission free

The core of the structure of this Museum was the old 'Iron Museum' (the 'Brompton Boilers') at South Kensington. There is a detailed account of its transformation in John Physick's book, *The Building of the Victoria & Albert Museum*, 1982. The iron structure of the Museum is remarkably delicate and the impression of space and light reinforces the colourful gaiety of the display of toys and games.

The Bethnal Green Museum was opened in 1872 as a branch of the South Kensington Museum with the intention of spreading the riches of that great institution to other less privileged parts of London. It was never planned as a local history museum; the specialist orientation towards childhood and children's interests only dates from 1915. The then director

Hand puppets, carved and painted by David Jones, *c*. 1922 (Bethnal Green Museum of Childhood)

realised that in wartime many schoolchildren who might have been able to go away to the country would be confined to London in the summer. Out of the activities and amusements organised for the children in the early years came the idea of a children's exhibition, which took place in 1923. From this grew a permanent 'Children's Section', which expanded under the patronage of Queen Mary. In 1974 the Museum was renamed to recognise the fact that it had become predominantly concerned with artefacts relating to childhood.

For many years there has also been a display of Continental decorative art, many pieces from 19thc International Exhibitions. Some of the more elaborate furniture is more ingenious than beautiful, but the examples of the Viennese Thonet's patent furniture are particularly interesting. All of this collection will eventually find its way to the Victoria and Albert Museum.

Of the main focus, there are about 4,000 toys in the collection: over 1,400 dolls, 60 complete dolls' houses, including the early 'Nuremberg' house of 1673, puppets and puppet theatres, including a complete 18thc Venetian marionette theatre and the recent acquisition of a rare example of artist-made hand puppets, carved and painted *c*. 1922 by David Jones for Eric Gill's children. There are at least 2,200 items of children's costume.

The Museum shop has a delightful stock calculated to interest the child visitors who are the Museum's principal public.

British Library

Manuscripts and printed books from all countries and in all languages (1500 BC–present day); extensive collection of early maps; large collection of printed and MS music

British Museum, Great Russell Street, London WC1
tel. 01-636 1544

Mon–Sat 10–5 pm; Sun 2.30–6 pm. Closed Christmas Eve–Boxing Day, New Year's Day, Good Fri and the May Bank Holiday

Admission free

Founded in 1973, the collection of the British Library was formed from the library departments of the British Museum and other library organisations and is housed within the British Museum itself. Only a very small proportion of the collection is on exhibition at any one time, but some of the most outstanding items in the Library's collections are on permanent display in the British Library galleries in the Museum—the Grenville Library, the Manuscript Saloon, the King's Library and the Map Gallery. Temporary exhibitions are regularly mounted in the Crawford Room, off the Manuscript Saloon.

The Western illuminated MSS are exhibited in the Grenville Library in two parts: MSS of English origin and those from the Continent. English examples shown include the Luttrell Psalter of *c*. 1340, the Evesham Psalter, the Rutland Psalter and the Psalter and Hours of Humphrey de Bohun, Earl of Hereford. On the Continental side, these range from the Harley Golden Gospels of about AD 800, probably made at the court of the Emperor Charlemagne, to richly illuminated Renaissance books from Italy and Flanders.

The Manuscript Saloon is primarily devoted to MSS of historical and literary interest. Famous items include two of the four surviving copies of King John's Magna Carta (1215) and the Lindisfarne Gospels (*c*. AD 698). Royal autographs are prominent among the historical letters and documents, and almost every major literary figure is represented in the section given to English literature. There are also displays of Bibles, heraldry, maps and music.

In the King's Library are illuminated MSS in Oriental languages, including Hebrew, from mediæval Europe, bibles and lectionaries of the Oriental Christian churches, illuminated Korans and Persian MSS, and palm leaves and paper from India and South-East Asia, as well as Chinese and Japanese printed books.

There is an exhibition of fine book-bindings from the 16thc to the present day, both British and Continental, and a case of documents and books on Shakespeare and displays of notable examples of book illustration from 1780 to 1960.

The history of printing is illustrated by notable early specimens, including the world's earliest dated example, the Diamond Sutra from China of AD 868. The forty-two-line Gutenberg Bible (*c*. 1455) and the first books printed in English and in the British Isles by William Caxton can also be seen. Displays on the history of music printing and of famous English children's books are shown.

In the Map Gallery the display of maps, charts, globes and atlases is changed periodically.

Small topical exhibitions from the collections of the Official Publications Library and the Newspaper Library are mounted from time to time.

The British Library Board is funded by the Office of Arts and Libraries and exercises authority under the British Library Act of 1972. It has close connections with the Friends of the National Libraries.

Marginal illumination from the Rutland Psalter, chess-players, 13thc–15thc (British Library)

British Museum

Antiquities: Oriental (i.e. China, India and Japan), Egyptian, Western Asiatic (i.e. Palestinian and Assyrian, etc.), Greek, Roman, Prehistoric and Romano-British, and Byzantine; fine and decorative works of art and archæology from the Middle Ages to the present day (Medieval and Later Antiquities); coins and medals; clocks and watches; the national collection of Western graphic art (Prints and Drawings Department)

Great Russell Street, London WC1
tel. 01-636 1555

Mon–Sat 10–5 pm; Sun 2.30–6 pm

Admission free, except for some special exhibitions

The statistics of the British Museum are awe-inspiring: the site itself covers no less than $11\frac{1}{2}$ acres and is visited by more than three million people in a year; in many of the departments the holdings are numbered in millions; twenty-five tons of paleolithic flints await the attentions of the rare specialists who wish to study them; the relatively recently-formed collection of American prints is the best outside America; the Egyptian collection is the largest outside Egypt; and, thanks to a recent bequest, the collection of Islamic pottery is the most representative anywhere; it is estimated that four centuries of man-hours will be needed to put all items in the Prints and Drawings Department onto a computerised register; the oven-baking of the vast collection of sun-dried Assyrian cuneiform tablets, a quarter of them from the Library of King Assurbanipal at Nineveh, has been going on for years and may take thirty more. Mere numbers cannot alone convey the flavour of this unique institution: faced with such riches and such diversity it is impossible to itemise all the noteworthy exhibits in the collections.

The present Museum grew out of a much more broadly based assemblage of every kind of rarity and curiosity, natural and artistic, amassed by the great antiquaries of the past. The names of the early patrons of the Museum constitute a roll-call of the most eminent, among them Sir Hans Sloane (1660–1753); the Tudor antiquary, Sir Robert Bruce Cotton (1571–1631); Sir Joseph Banks (1743–1820); Sir William Hamilton (part of whose vast collection was bought in 1772); Lord Elgin (of the Elgin marbles); Charles Towneley (whose collection came to the Museum in 1805); Richard Payne Knight (1750–1824); the great 19thc archæologist, Sir Henry Layard, and many others. Their collections ranged over the finest antiquities, from the Elgin Marbles and the Bassae frieze to the famous Towneley Marbles; the sculptures from Nimrud, the lost city of the Assyrians rediscovered by Layard; the most impressive books and manuscripts, notably the twelve thousand volumes from the old Royal Library presented by King George II, which had been built up by the sovereigns of England since the 15thc; large collections of natural curiosities and ethnographic items, as well as coinage, medals, and even postage stamps from the massive collection of King George V.

The British Museum was founded, like the National Gallery, as the result of a purchase, in this case the library and collections of artistic and natural curiosities amassed by Sir Hans Sloane, which in accordance with his will were offered to the Nation in 1753 for £20,000, although they had cost him, it was estimated, £50,000 and were said to be worth £80,000. To the Sloane Collection were added the Cotton and Harley libraries, after an act of Parliament in 1753. The money for these purchases and for the procuring of a building in which to house these treasures was raised by a lottery. At that moment Montagu House in Great Russell Street became available on very liberal terms, and the house being repaired and the appropriate cabinets and bookshelves having been installed, the new British Museum opened to the public in January 1759. The whole expenditure on the premises amounted to less than £30,000, as an Account from the Trustees shows: £10,250 for the purchase of Montagu House, £14,484 for repairs, £4,076 for furniture, etc., down to £140 for fire engines.

Apart from the very important collections of antique sculpture housed in the Townley and Elgin galleries and the fine historical manuscripts, books and charters from Hans Sloane, Burleigh's state papers and the Lansdowne Collection, a great part of the display was once given over to 'a miscellaneous collection of articles from all parts of the world, arranged, as nearly as possible, in geographical order' (*Synopsis of the Contents of the British Museum*, 1808).

Thirty thousand of the 'natural curiosities' came from Sir Hans Sloane's collection; but the exhibits accumulated rapidly, from Captain Cook (through Sir Joseph Banks), among others, who brought back numerous items from the South Sea Islands, Australasia and North America, and there were also exhibits of mineral ores, lavas and other geological specimens taken from 'a large store deposited in a less conspicuous part of the house' (see *Public Buildings in London*, 1823). The Trustees had also purchased 'Greenwood's collection of stuffed birds', which would have looked perfectly appropriate to a display that also included stuffed giraffes. At the very time when the description to accompany Augustus Pugin's illustrations of Montagu House for *The Public Buildings of London* was being written, Robert Smirke (1781–1867) was already at work on extensions to the house and in the autumn of 1823 the first tenders were sought for the progressive reconstruction of the Museum buildings by Smirke. The final result is the great neo-classical building that we know today; the façade is practically